Grimsby
Docks

IN OLD PHOTOGRAPHS

An ice barque and steam paddle tug passing through the 70 ft lock towards the Royal
Dock.

Grimsby
Docks

IN OLD PHOTOGRAPHS

JANET TIERNEY

Alan Sutton Publishing Limited
Phoenix Mill · Far Thrupp · Stroud
Gloucestershire

First Published 1994

British Library Cataloguing in Publication Data.
A catalogue record for this book is available from
the British Library.

ISBN 0–7509–0759–2

Typeset in 9/10 Sabon.
Typesetting and origination by
Alan Sutton Publishing Limited.
Printed in Great Britain by
The Guernsey Press Company Limited,
Guernsey, Channel Islands.

Contents

A. Maclure's *Bird's Eye View of Great Grimsby Docks*, drawn *c.* 1880. The Royal Dock, crowded with shipping, occupies the centre of the drawing, and a steamer can be seen passing through the newly built Union Dock. Further sailing ships can be seen in the Alexandra Dock, of which there is as yet only one arm. On the far right is the Fish Dock. Because the Dock Company at that time did not grant building leases, the smack owners and fish merchants inhabited a series of temporary buildings near the pontoon.

Introduction

Grimsby's origins as a port stretch back to the pre-Conquest Viking settlement around its haven, one of the Humber's many tidal creeks. At the time of the Norman Conquest, Grimsby had a substantial trade with Norway, and by the early thirteenth century it was an east coast port of modest importance – a long way behind the major ports such as Boston, Hull and King's Lynn, but well ahead of Yarmouth, Barton and many others.

In 1986 an excavation in the old Baxtergate car park by the Humberside Archaeological Unit revealed the line of the fourteenth-century waterfront of the medieval port, which appeared to correspond with the line of what is now the remains of South Dock Street. This was the heart of the trading area of the medieval port, and, as the excavation further revealed, it was still so in the eighteenth century. As well as the traditional trade with Norway, the Newcastle Chamberlains' Accounts in the early sixteenth century record the existence of an important coastal trade in coal from there to Grimsby. Between 1508 and 1511, for example, the *Thomas, Cristoffer, Mawdlen* and other Grimsby vessels regularly sailed from Newcastle laden with chauldrons of 'collis' for the haven.

During the sixteenth century the haven declined. Gradual silting meant that even in the early sixteenth century the larger colliers were unable to moor at the Riverhead, and had to be berthed in the marshes towards the mouth of the haven. Timber from Norwegian ships was brought ashore in barges, while the ships lay off the coast in the Humber. Grimsby was caught in a vicious circle – silting of the haven killed the shipping trade and impoverished the town, while the very poverty of the town meant that the decay and silting of the haven could not be addressed. By the seventeenth century, the port subsisted on infrequent coastal traffic which was forced to moor away from the Riverhead.

Various efforts were made to improve the haven and resurrect the prosperity of the port, but it was not until the end of the eighteenth century that a step of any significance was taken. In 1796 the Grimsby Haven Act was passed '. . . for Widening, Deepening, Enlarging, Altering and Improving the Haven of the Town and Port of Great Grimsby . . .', and John Rennie, one of the leading civil engineering lights of the day, was invited to prepare plans for a new diversion of the River Freshney into the haven, and the construction of a proper dock with a lock entrance. Despite many problems, not the least being that the entire work took place while the Napoleonic Wars were in full swing, the dock was finally opened in November 1801. This Old Dock, as it was later known, is still in existence, forming the upper arm of the Alexandra Dock and feeding into the Riverhead.

While it was a vast improvement on what had previously existed, the Old Dock suffered from various problems, not least of which was the difficulty in entering it in any but the most favourable sea conditions. Despite this, sea-borne trade gradually increased, bringing modest prosperity and resulting in the development of ancillary activities such as ship-building in the port. The real stimulus to Grimsby's fortunes came with the amalgamation of three smaller railway companies and the new Grimsby

Docks Company to form the remarkably forward-looking and highly ambitious Manchester, Sheffield and Lincolnshire Railway.

The MS & LR appointed the extremely distinguished James Meadows Rendel as engineer responsible for the planned new docks, which were visualized as a port complex large enough to compete with Hull. The dock entrance was designed to be beyond the low water mark to allow ships to use it at any tide, and Rendel reclaimed the 1,000 ft long basin from the Humber by building a vast coffer dam of Baltic timber. The first pile that was driven in 1846 went straight into quicksand and promptly disappeared – not a very favourable commencement, as a contemporary commentator acidly remarked – but the entire project, successfully completed in 1852 at a cost of over £1 million, is still regarded as one of the three greatest engineering achievements of Rendel's glittering career.

The Royal Dock's principal trade was in coal and timber, although the latter was very seasonal, resulting in considerable unemployment in the town during the winter. Trade rapidly outgrew dock space, and in 1873 more room was provided by making a 100 ft wide cut, the Union Dock, linking the Old and Royal Docks. Even this proved insufficient, particularly with the rise in grain imports through the port in the 1870s, and a 26 acre extension was built to the Old and Union Docks to form the Alexandra Dock, completed in 1884. The MS & LR's speculation in revivifying a moribund port had paid off spectacularly: Grimsby had become the fifth largest port in Britain by the end of the century.

By the 1840s fishing boats from the south and south-west were exploiting the new grounds discovered in the North Sea, and the construction of a rail link to London encouraged many of these smacks to use Grimsby to land their catches. However, it was the MS & LR's creation of a fish dock to the east of the Royal Dock in 1857 which really enabled the fishing industry in the port to take off. Within two years the company was being pressurized to create more space, but a second dock was not started until 1866. By 1882 the writer of the Grimsby section of Kelly's *Directory* could state confidently that '. . . the fishing trade of this port exceeds and has a larger area of dock space allotted to it than any other port in the kingdom'.

The boost given to the industry by the adoption of the steam trawlers lead to the MS & LR's successors, the Great Central, obtaining an Act of Parliament to construct a third dock. War and escalating post-war costs meant that the work was deferred until 1930, and was begun then only after the Corporation of Grimsby borrowed money to build it themselves with the aid of a government grant, leasing it back to the railway company.

Today, nearly a century and a half after the first fish dock was built, Grimsby's fishing industry is in ruins. Over-fishing, the unilateral extension of territorial waters into traditional grounds, and political pusillanimity in the European Union have all paid their part in its demise. In 1985 the end of deep-sea trawling was marked by the sale of the last eleven surviving 'Cat' class side-winder trawlers by British United Trawlers for work as oil rig standby vessels. What remains is nostalgia. But nostalgia should not cloud the fact that the fishing industry was built from the courage and skill of generations of Grimsby men who worked, often in truly dreadful conditions, in an industry statistically more dangerous even than coal mining, nor that these men were all too readily exploited and ignored both by owners and by governments.

The photographs in this book have been chosen to reflect the work of both the commercial and the fish docks from the early 1860s to the 1980s, and of the many industries and activities which the existence of the docks supported. Many, particularly those of the fish docks and the fishing fleet, were taken by people who actually worked there – the fishermen, shipyard workers and office staff.

The Royal Dock

The Royal Dock at Grimsby, depicted under construction in the elegant painting by J.W. Carmichael. The dock, built on land reclaimed from the Humber foreshore, was designed by one of Britain's leading civil engineers of the day, James Meadows Rendel, with Adam Smith of Brigg as resident-engineer.

Rendel's magnificent Dock Tower, 309 ft in height, *c.* 1862. The tower dominated the entrance to the Royal Dock and contained the accumulator for the hydraulic engines and cranes on the dockside, and provided the power to open the lock gates. Adam Smith's machinery inside the tower also provided fresh water for shipping in the dock – at the rate of one shilling per ton when this photograph was taken!

The first coal jetty on the Royal Dock, pictured in the 1870s. Grimsby had been trading in coal intermittently since at least the sixteenth century, but the large-scale export of coal from the Yorkshire, Nottinghamshire and Derbyshire coalfields had grown exponentially with the construction of the new dock. By the time this photograph was taken, around 300,000 tons per year was passing out of the port. The coal drops on this jetty could load a ship with a thousand tons of coal a day.

Grimsby's great advantage over up-river Hull in the nineteenth century was that it had suitable water to keep alive fish caught by well-smacks until they were sold. By 1858 smacks had started using ice at sea, cut from ponds and stored in a thatched ice house on the docks. In 1857 the first ice barques arrived from Norway, carrying ice from the Scandinavian lakes. This is the *Effendi* from Breveg, photographed around 1870.

Ice barques moored in the Royal Dock; the tarpaulin is covering damage to the ship's bows. With the production of commercial ice in Grimsby, the ice trade gradually faltered until the First World War effectively extinguished it. The photograph was taken by H. Watkinson in around 1902.

The Dock Tower was – and remains – *the* landmark of Grimsby. As Tessyman's 1852 *Directory and Handbook* for the town put it: 'Coming along the railway, from London or from Hull, from Manchester or from Lincoln, this tower strikes your eye as the only prominent building distinguishable from the general mass . . .' The writer concludes, with somewhat smug local chauvinism, '. . . [it] surpasses by fifty feet the loftiest pinnacle of any kind that Hull can boast of . . .'.

A steamer passing through the 70 ft lock into the Royal Dock in the 1870s.

Shipping in the Royal Dock, c. 1893. Among the vessels in the foreground, on the right in front of the Tower, are the barque *Warden Law*, the barquentine *Violet* in the centre, and the topsail schooner *Pride of Anglesey* from Beaumaris on the far left.

The grain barque *Port Jackson* under tow in the Humber. Grain was a fairly significant import through the Royal Dock. When the Royal Dock first opened, wheat destined for the industrial north was being brought in from France, while the importation of cheap grain from California in the 1870s and '80s was considered to be contributing to the agricultural depression apparent in Britain by the mid-1870s. By the early twentieth century much of the wheat came from Russia, harvested and processed by the very machinery that had originally been shipped out there through Grimsby from Lincoln and Gainsborough!

The Dock Tower from the herring slip and tidal basin. The small castellated building on the right was an auxiliary tower to provide supplementary hydraulic power. The building behind it was the old Royal Dock station, built to receive Queen Victoria in 1854, and converted in around 1870 into a temporary hostel for emigrants en route to Liverpool and the United States. The photograph was taken by William Garthwaite, a local professional photographer, around 1890.

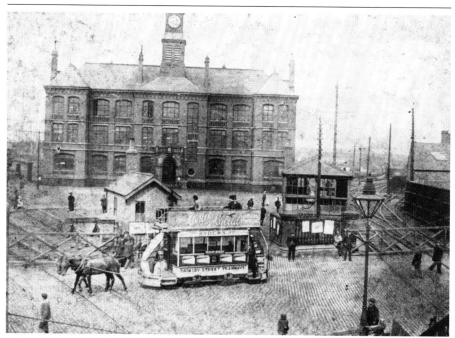

The Dock Crossing and Dock Offices, *c.* 1902. The foundation stone of the office building was laid by Sir Thomas Fremantle in 1873; it opened for business in 1875.

The Royal Dock Hotel (to give it its full title) was built by John Brown of Grimsby next to the Dock Crossing in 1864–5. A handsome building in what the Victorians referred to as the 'Italian style', it catered for the well-heeled visitors who came to Grimsby by rail and sea. It also attracted the attentions of riotous locals, as seen here in the aftermath of an election disturbance in 1877.

Grimsby Dock Police, outside the Dock Offices in 1905. The Dock Police were a separate body from the Borough Police, being under the direction of the railway company.

LNER.POLICE FORCE.GRIMSBY DOCKS

Grimsby Dock Police Force in 1930, near the site of the proposed new No. 3 Fish Dock. A retired naval officer, Captain F.A. Richardson, who compiled a social survey of the town in 1936, noted with approval that one of the duties of these policemen was to guard every road or pathway into the dock estate, gated or otherwise, to form a sort of *cordon sanitaire* between it and the rest of the town.

The officers and men of HMS *Ariel* relaxing on board their ship at Grimsby. The picture dates from the late nineteenth century, the *Ariel* in question being either the gunboat that was sold off in 1889 or the destroyer that was launched in 1897 and wrecked ten years later.

HMS *Grimsby*, a 990-ton sloop, heading out into the Humber after making her first and highly successful visit to the town in June 1934. Her naval career was short but illustrious, serving in engagements off Greece, Cyprus and Libya before being sunk off Tobruk while defending a convoy.

Visit to Immingham July 22 nd 1912. The King & Queen Board ng S.S. Killingholme

King George V and Queen Mary boarding the Great Central Railway's most recent Humber ferry, the *Killingholme*, at the Royal Dock, en route to opening the railway company's most recent dock facility at Immingham on 22 July 1912. *Killingholme* was to carry far less exalted passengers (sheep) on the Humber only a few years later. She was commandeered by the Admiralty to take seaplanes out into the North Sea to shoot down Zeppelins, but the venture ended in ignominious failure when she was torpedoed in the paddle – by a fishing boat! She limped back to Grimsby and her voyages henceforth were confined to the Humber. This was probably just as well, since one of her small design faults was a compass which resolutely pointed to the funnel regardless of the direction of travel.

Divers were required for routine maintenance work on the lock gates and dock facilities, as well as for coping with any underwater hazards or accidental damage to the dock or shipping in it. The divers in these two photographs, which date from just before the First World War, were supplied with air from a manually operated portable pump either on board ship or on the dock side.

The Grimsby lifeboat showing its paces to a crowd in the tidal basin outside the entrance to the Royal Dock at the turn of the century. The lifeboat was originally based at Cleethorpes, but because of launching difficulties it was moved to Grimsby in 1887, and eventually, in 1907, to Spurn. The photograph was taken by William Garthwaite.

Henry Etherington, an employee of the Great Central Railway Company and a member of the St John's swimming club in Grimsby, evidently made a habit of diving from great heights into the Royal Dock. Having already dived off the side of a ship and a small crane, Mr Etherington climbed to the top of a 100 ft crane near the lock pits, and plunged through the air '. . . amid vociferous cheers of a big crowd, including many naval men', according to the awe-struck reporter of the event from the *Grimsby News*.

The Dock Master, complete with speaking trumpet, striding purposefully past the lock gates at the base of the Dock Tower, *c*. 1910.

Captain Alfred Cook, the Lock Master, with two companions, *c.* 1937.

Mr J. Bottomley, the Royal Dock gateman, was responsible for operating the locks at either side of the Dock Tower. The photograph was taken in 1966 by Roland Burton of Grimsby.

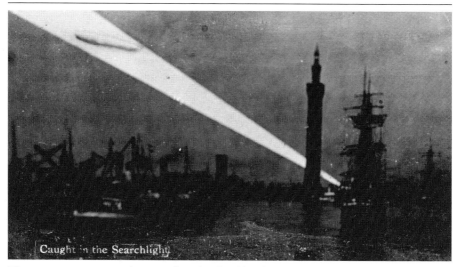

Caught in the Searchlight

The east coast towns and ports of England suffered during the First World War from the unwelcome attentions of the German Zeppelin airships. Grimsby was no exception: in 1915, when this monster was caught over the Royal Dock, it suffered a raid in which seventeen bombs were dropped on Scartho, fortunately without loss of life.

The Great Central Railway steamer *Dewsbury* leaving the Royal Dock for the Continent. *Dewsbury* was one of five sister-ships (the others being *Accrington*, *Stockport*, *Blackburn*, and *Bury*) that sailed between Grimsby, Hamburg, Rotterdam and Antwerp. Built in 1890 by the Manchester, Sheffield and Lincolnshire Railway, she remained in service until 1959, interrupted only by war service between 1914 and 1918 as an Admiralty store carrier, and as an Admiralty rescue ship between 1939 and 1945.

The *City of Leeds* was launched on 8 June 1897 by the Lady Mayoress of Leeds, and was used by the Great Central Railway Company to operate their passenger and cargo service between the Royal Dock and the Continent. Despite excellent passenger facilities, she lacked a wireless, and thus could not be contacted after leaving Grimsby in August 1914. The steamer spent the war interned in Kiel and was used as a minelaying depot ship, while her unfortunate crew languished in the Ruhleben camp near Berlin. After the war she was returned, and operated her old service under the LNER until 1935, when she was declared redundant, and was broken up at Blyth the following year.

Fruit was a significant import through the Royal Dock in the 1930s; here the fruit boat is being unloaded on the east side of the dock. It is interesting to see that while produce is being craned off the ship, some fruit is also being unloaded in wicker baskets, as fish were. The photograph was taken by S.J. Warren of Grimsby.

Shipping on the east side of the Royal Dock, *c.* 1960.

Poised over the dock side, a new diesel engine manufactured by Ruston's of Lincoln waits to be swung out and into the engine room of the Grimsby trawler *Lucerne*.

Dredging at the entrance to the tidal basin in the 1930s. The photographer was Jack Jones, then a ship repairer with E. Bacon & Co.

The west side of the Royal Dock, photographed in January 1959 by Roland Burton.

Paper from Dixon's mills in Grimsby being loaded into the hold of a vessel on the west side of the dock in the mid-1960s. The raw material for this paper ('newsprint', for printing newspapers) was wood pulp from Scandinavia, which was imported into Grimsby in large quantities.

Grain streaming into the hold of a cargo vessel, *c.* 1965. The photograph, taken from a glass plate negative, is one of a series commissioned from local professional Roland Burton during the 1960s, covering commercial activity in the ports of Grimsby and Immingham.

The Lynn Well lightship moored on the east side of the dock. Her usual home was off the coast of South Lincolnshire, near the Wash.

A car being loaded into a ship's hold early in March 1941.

Sacks of malt produced by United British Maltsters of Newark being craned on board for export during the late 1950s. The photographer was Roland Burton.

The Sail Training Association's vessel *Malcolm Miller* during a visit to Grimsby in July 1981.

SECTION TWO

Alexandra Dock and the Riverhead

Morning mist on the Riverhead, and cargoes stacked on the quayside at Blow's landing stage, *c.* 1925.

Grain being unloaded from a Humber sloop at Marshall's mill on the Riverhead in the latter part of the nineteenth century. In the foreground, planks of timber can be seen seasoning in the water.

A cod-smack under construction at Collinsons' Yard near the Riverhead in the 1880s. Collinsons' was one of no less than eleven shipbuilders working in the port in the early 1880s; but changing times were indicated by the existence of two yards specializing in the construction of iron vessels.

George and Thomas Collinson, photographed in the 1880s. The Collinsons had an excellent reputation for building sturdy and well designed fishing smacks in their yard on the Old Dock.

Haven Street, *c.* 1920, was one of the now-demolished little commercial streets that ran up to the Riverhead. At the far end of the street was the old custom-house, which became redundant when the Dock Offices were built in 1873.

The Riverhead busy with river traffic, photographed from Victoria Street in 1919. Sowerby's mill and the West Haven warehouses can be seen on the right.

Looking up the Riverhead towards the Alexandra Dock. The River Freshney enters the dock just before Mitchell's builders' merchants. The warehouses on the left, in what was South Dock Street, have now all been demolished, along with Blow's offices.

The *Basalt* and her sister-ship *Quenast*, both owned by Blow's, carried goods daily across the Humber between the Oberon Wharf in Hull and the Riverhead.

Unloading goods from the *Basalt* at Blow's landing stage, with Sowerby's Victoria Street premises in the background. The Riverhead was a major commercial centre until the twentieth century, lined with mills and maltings; but as the coastal trade diminished, so the Riverhead became, quite literally, a backwater.

A square-rigged Humber keel, once a familiar sight in the Riverhead, cutting its way past other shipping in the river, and heading towards Grimsby in September 1902.

The staple trades of the port of Grimsby, up until the coming of the fishing smacks in the 1850s, had for long been coal and timber, the latter with the Baltic countries and with Russia. Although trade with Russia was severely disrupted by the Crimean War, its rapid recovery after the peace of 1856, combined with the general increase in commercial activity, meant that the Royal Dock was seriously stretched. Accordingly, improvements were made, initially by connecting the Old and Royal Docks with the Union Dock in 1873–4, and by awarding a contract in late 1878 to Messrs Logan & Hemingway to construct the eastern extension to the Old Dock, linking the two together to form the Alexandra Dock.

Timber and shipping together in the Alexandra Dock at the end of the nineteenth century.

Planks from the timber ship *St Helens* being stacked against the sides of the vessel in the Alexandra Dock. The photograph was taken around 1920.

An unidentified naval visitor to the Alexandra Dock in 1910. Grimsby had a long association with the Royal Navy, including the less than desirable reputation of being a good source of men in the days of the press-gang, when fishermen were stopped and 'pressed' while their boats were still in the Humber. In less troubled times, the Navy regarded the port as a popular 'run ashore'.

The rear of Marshall's (later Spiller's) mill, facing on to the Alexandra Dock, with Humber keels tied up alongside. The mill was one of the largest flour mills in the country at the time that this photograph was taken (just before the First World War), and processed some of the American and Eastern European grain imported into Grimsby through the Royal Dock.

Spiller's Mill in the 1980s, with small inshore fishing boats moored at its rear. The mill, compared with the photograph on the opposite page, shows the ravages of the various serious fires which have befallen it during the course of the century.

The Corporation Road swing bridge, 283 ft long, linked Freeport Wharf on Victoria Street and the West Marsh across Alexandra Dock. It was built under an Act of Parliament of 1869, opened to the public in 1873, and caused nothing but trouble thereafter. It was, however, of immense importance in facilitating the development of the West Marsh for both housing and commerce.

The much-reviled Corporation Road swing bridge in its last days in the early 1920s, looking over the Alexandra Dock into Central Market and Victoria Street.

The swing bridge in action in the early 1920s.

Sir William Arrol's 1928 lifting bridge, raised to allow a small steamer to pass down Alexandra Dock towards the Humber.

The new Corporation Road lifting bridge and the extensive timber yards, bounded by Alexandra Road on the right, and stretching up to the Riverhead in the distance. The photograph was taken on 8 August 1940 from the roof of Spiller's grain silo in Victoria Street.

In the 1930s the timber industry and paper producers were the only large-scale employers in the town outside the fishing industry. By the 1960s, when this photograph of the deal yards at Alexandra Dock was taken, the situation had already begun to change. New and diverse industries were providing increasing employment opportunities all along the Humber Bank, and the timber yards were set to contract drastically, leaving acres of derelict land on both sides of the dock.

British and French matelots exhibiting some post-Entente Cordiale *fraternité* on Corporation Bridge, *c.* 1907.

In 1908 Grimsby was visited by the new 'C' class submarines. C2, on the left, was commanded by Lieutenant Arthur Jameson, heir to the Irish whiskey fortune. The railway wagons belong to Edward Bannister & Co., and are full of coal for shipping.

Captain Richardson, in his 1936 survey of Grimsby, found that in the densely populated area around the docks there were 182 people per public house (compared with 2,300 in the leafy suburbs). The Packet Tavern, which stood on the corner of King Street and New Dock Street was one such pub, and took its name from the nearby landing stage in the Union Dock for the steam packets from Hull and elsewhere.

Robert Blow, wharfinger, warehouseman, steamship and sloop owner, photographed in 1891 outside his house in Haven Street, close by his landing stage. The family firm had been carrying goods across and down the Humber and Trent since before Waterloo.

SECTION THREE
The Fish Docks

A bird's-eye view of the Fish Docks, taken from the top of the Dock Tower by Stanley Warren in the late 1920s. No. 1 Fish Dock and the two small graving docks are to the left; No. 2 Dock is over to the right. The waves breaking on the Humber Bank in the distance mark the site of the third, yet-to-be-built, dock.

Steam herring drifters tied up at the herring slip, which was actually part of the tidal basin at the entrance to the Royal Dock, rather than the Fish Docks proper.

Smacks tied up in No. 1 Fish Dock, *c.* 1870, before the advent of steam power to the fishing fleet.

FISH DOCK, GRIMSBY.

Steam trawlers in No. 2 Fish Dock, *c.* 1920.

Landing herrings from drifters on the herring slip in the tidal basin at the end of the nineteenth century. Although Grimsby, unlike Great Yarmouth and Lowestoft, was predominantly a white fish port, from the middle of August until about the end of October it enjoyed the bustle of the herring drifters as they followed the shoals down the east coast.

Unloading the catch in the traditional manner from the stern of a smack on to a wet quayside in the early 1870s.

Days of plenty . . . fish laid out on No. 2 Fish Pontoon before the First World War.

Serried ranks of cod laid out on Henderson's Jetty Pontoon on No. 2 Fish Dock. The photograph was one of several of the Pontoon taken by Stanley Warren of Ainslie Street in the early 1930s.

Steam trawlers being unloaded at the Pontoon in the 1920s.

A lumper on the Pontoon hooking a wicker fish basket across a plank from the trawler's side to the quay.

Lumpers – the so-called 'midnight millionaires', a reference to their ability to earn potentially large wages for hard labouring at very unsocial hours – unloading fish in the traditional wicker baskets in January 1959.

This singularly unappealing creature baring its formidable dentition to the camera is a monkfish, or angler, a bottom-dwelling creature which burrows into the mud on the sea-bed and lures unsuspecting smaller fish into its capacious jaws. It has even been known to grab the odd seagull at low tide. Unsurprisingly, it is *always* sold headless. Monkfish, however, belie their hideous appearance, being exquisitely sweet-flavoured with a succulent texture. The photograph was taken in 1950.

Captain W.R. Baxter, Dock Master for the Manchester, Sheffield and Lincolnshire Railway, *c.* 1890. By the end of the century, both the Royal and the Fish Docks had their own Dock Master, that for the Fish Docks being the senior appointment.

Coaling a trawler by horse and cart at the end of the nineteenth century. Until the hydraulic coal drop was built in No. 2 Fish Dock in 1892, coal had to be brought round to the fish docks either in lighters or by cart.

Coal being mechanically bunkered directly into a trawler using the newly installed coal drop.

In the early 1930s, when the new fish dock was opened, the fishing industry in Grimsby was devouring about one million tons of best large steam coal from the Yorkshire coalfields annually. To cope with this consumption efficiently, the new dock was provided with six coaling berths equipped with three state-of-the-art mechanical hoists, whose buckets could bunker trawlers at a rate of between 60 and 80 tons per hour.

Trawlers coaling in No. 3 Fish Dock in the early 1950s. The photograph was taken by Fred Brewster, a well-known local amateur photographer and former president of Grimsby Photographic Society.

Not all fish caught is sent for auction. Poor quality, small or otherwise undesirable fish are converted to fish meal for a variety of agricultural purposes; even perfectly good fish could meet this fate if there was a strike of shore-workers delaying landing, or if fish prices were too depressed to make selling on the market worthwhile. This photograph, taken in the 1960s, shows 'waste' fish being loaded on to the Grimsby Fish Meal Company's lorries for their factory at Pyewipe.

The paddle steamer *Humber* was built in 1876, and was used mainly for towing fishing smacks and other sailing vessels out into the Humber, or, if the winds were unfavourable, right out into the North Sea itself.

The *Stanley Africanus*, owned by W.W. Crampin's, *c.* 1910.

A dock worker crossing the old swing bridge between Nos 1 and 2 Fish Docks. The bridge was removed in 1962 to widen the cutting.

The Pontoon, photographed from the corner of Fish Dock Road in the early 1950s.

The 1901 lock-out lasted fourteen weeks, caused immense hardship to the fishermen and their families, and led to a full-scale riot and three naval gunboats being despatched to lie off the port. It was the latest in a series of industrial disputes in the docks, and centred on the trawler owners' decision to pay crews a share wage, the existing practice for skippers and mates, rather than a weekly wage. When the dispute finally ended, both sides claimed victory, although the reality of the situation was that the fishermen ultimately gained very little.

Fishermen signing a petition outside Consolidated Fisheries' premises to press for the inclusion of share fishermen – by this date, everyone from skippers to deckhands – in the 1906 Workmen's Compensation Act. The difficulties in unionizing the Grimsby fishermen has historically left them extremely vulnerable to the actions of both the owners and central government. Their needs and aspirations have all too frequently been ignored.

Piling the lock entrance tie beams for the new No. 3 Fish Dock in April 1932.

Work on the new dock was severely disrupted by spring storms – the embankment was actually breached and a considerable amount of the chalk bank washed away. This photograph by Sid Burton shows workmen repairing the gap on May Day 1932.

The wall of the lock entrance to the new dock under construction in September 1932. The construction of the local entrance involved the use of 560 tons of steel sheet piling, the placing of 18,400 cubic yards of concrete, and the setting of 18,000 cubic feet of granite.

Work in progress in May 1933 on the slipways and South Quay. The quays were a problem area because of the soft ground encountered while working on them. New designs for them had to be prepared to take this into account and different methods of construction adopted, both of which caused several months' delay to the work.

Trawlers at the fitting-out berths in No. 3 Fish Dock, photographed *c.* 1935 by Stanley Warren.

Trawlers in No. 2 Graving Dock in the 1930s. In the foreground is the *Sisapon*.

On 14 June 1943 the fish docks were attacked by German bombers. Incendiary bombs dropped between Fish Dock Road and No. 2 Dock's wooden fish market led to a huge conflagration in Hutton Road, Cross Street, Wharncliffe Road and Auckland Road, so intense that trawlers moored by the fish market had to be hastily moved out into the dock. These two photographs show the skeletal remains in the aftermath of the raid.

Trawlers ice-bound in Grimsby during the exceptionally hard winter of 1947.

Inshore sailing vessels sheltering at Grimsby during another bitter winter, that of 1962/3.

Fishermen arriving by taxi to the trawlers tied up along the North Wall in the late 1950s.

A sight which symbolized Grimsby to the rest of the world: the North Wall packed with trawlers preparing to sail, c. 1962.

Four distant-water trawlers – *Ross Dainty, Hondo, Judaean* and *Ross Tiger* – on the fish dock slipway in the early 1970s. In the distance are the chimneys of Grimsby's twentieth-century industrial developments following the curve of the Humber Bank towards Immingham in the far distance.

Salsbury's Café, otherwise known as 'Solly's', on the herring slip near the entrance to the Royal Dock, in the early 1960s.

Kenneth Younger, MP for Grimsby, deep in an early morning conversation with lumpers in their canteen on the fish docks in the early 1950s.

The Queen and Prince Philip on board the Onward Steam Fishing Company's trawler *Rhodesian* in the course of an official visit to Grimsby, Saturday 28 June 1958.

Wolverhampton Wanderers tied up at the Pontoon in the late 1950s. Built in Beverley in 1946 as one of the first oil-burning steam trawlers, and originally named the *St Matthew*, she was bought by Consolidated Fisheries in December 1956 and renamed as part of their 'football' fleet. The following year she was involved in the dramatic rescue of the crew of a merchant ship, the *Bosworth*, in appalling weather and sea conditions.

Ever-hopeful seagulls waiting alongside the small seine-netters tied up at a wet Pontoon, *c*. 1990. The Pontoon buildings were scheduled for demolition in 1993, but were provisionally added to the DoE list as being worthy of preservation. However, they were removed from the list, and demolition finally started towards the end of the year.

SECTION FOUR
Ancillary Industries

The cowls of the smoke-house chimneys on Grimsby Docks, photographed in 1978 by David Armstrong ARPS.

During the herring season the Scots fisher girls were a familiar sight on the herring slip, gutting and packing the fish in brine into wooden casks, ready for export to Germany and the Low Countries. The girls worked outside in all weathers, standing in groups of three, processing anything up to a thousand fish an hour. They commanded a considerable reputation for toughness and hard work; even when relaxing (below) their hands were never still.

Grimsby was long famous for producing clean-cut fillets, which gave the customer a minimum of waste. Tommy Far (bottom left) had a reputation on the docks as a miraculously fast and precise filleter. He is shown here, in around 1937, with colleagues Bert Hughes (right) and Ginger Agason (above right).

Three young ladies from H. Smethurst's Ltd, the fish curers, taken either at their Pontoon or Ropery Street premises in 1931. The girl on the left of the trio is Doll Brown.

Examining haddock to ascertain the extent of the 'cure' at Ernest Cox & Co.'s smoke-house. Unlike cod, which are cured in long strips, haddock are split and immersed for ten to fifteen minutes in a brine solution, then drained from a rod known as a 'speight'. In the 1950s, when this photograph was taken, the speights of fish were hung in a vertical smoke-house over a smouldering fire of oak and whitewood sawdust, the traditional method of curing. The time taken varied with the weather; modern curing is carried out in computer-controlled horizontal kilns.

Salting and drying as a means of preserving fish is a centuries-old process. In the 1930s over a hundred acres of open country round Grimsby was devoted to the drying of salted cod by sun and wind for export to the Mediterranean and Latin America. The photograph above was taken at Fretwell's fish curers in Fish House Lane, now subsumed into Ladysmith Road. Below, also pictured before the First World War, are a group of workers at the fish salting nets in David Street.

The whole industry revolved around the sale of fish, since prices affected not just the fishermen themselves, but also the army of ancillary workers and ultimately the town's tradesmen. In few other industries did the subtle barometer of consumer taste, or the complex laws of supply and demand, have so immediate or potentially devastating an effect on the community. Fish merchants watched the landings so that by 7.30 a.m., when the sales started, they had already assessed the quality and quantity to be sold. The fish were laid out in squares, and the boxes sold from them. The picture above was taken on the Pontoon around 1960, that below, some ten years later.

Cod is a large fish, although this is not generally apparent to those whose only acquaintance with the creature are the modest and manageable fillets found neatly packed in polystyrene trays in supermarket chillers; this one, caught around 1930, is of heroic proportions. It gives some idea as to why the catching of cod is so gruelling an occupation.

Process workers at Sleight's at the turn of the century.

Appleyard's workers – and purchases – photographed at their premises at the north end of the Pontoon.

Thomas Stattersfield, fish merchant on the Pontoon, photographed at the rear of his home at 87 Lord Street, *c*. 1892.

W.H. (Bill) Harrison, who operated from Chapman's Pontoon in the mid-1930s.

Landing and packing fish ready for the morning market from small inshore vessels at the north end of the Pontoon in the mid-1930s.

The staff of the Great Central Railway's fish department, *c.* 1900.

Railway wagons full of fish ready for distribution. In the 1930s, when this photograph was taken, Grimsby was distributing its fish by express train to all parts of Great Britain so effectively that it was being sold in the shops the morning after it had been landed.

George Waumsley (seated), his sons Norman (left) and Frank (right) and an unknown boy assistant with his fish van. Mr Waumsley supplied fresh Grimsby fish from his shop at 32 St Peter's Avenue, and despatched bass bags – square carrier bags made of plaited bass (a grass) filled with fish and ice, and stitched across the top – to, as his van advertises, all parts of the country as requested.

Packing fish fillets for despatch to inland distributors, 1956. The wooden box was lined with greaseproof paper, iced at the bottom, and the fish iced again half-way through the box. A second layer of greaseproof paper covered the final fish layer, further ice was added, and the box nailed down. The melting ice trickled down through the fish layers during transit, maintaining a cool temperature until the fish reached its destination.

By 1955, when this photograph was taken, Grimsby had the largest quick-freezing industry in the United Kingdom. These women are seen weighing fillets prior to their being frozen.

T. Baskcomb's ropery works on Fish Dock Road, *c.* 1910. The manager, Billy Forman, is seated top left. Rope-making was not a mechanized process at this date – the dressed hemp was drawn out by the spinners walking backwards while a boy turned a wheel binding the strands together. Many of the terraces in the Ladysmith and Welholme Road district had long areas between their back gardens which housed small rope-walks.

In 1868, about five years before this photograph was taken, C. Cottam was one of only four rope-makers working in Grimsby itself. The dramatic growth of the fishing industry in the last quarter of the nineteenth century is illustrated by the fact that by 1906 this number had more than quadrupled to seventeen. Cottam's rope-works were in Clee Lane, the shop in Victoria Street, on the site of the present-day Woolworths.

By as early as 1906 the Great Grimsby Coal, Salt and Tanning Company (or Cosalt, as it came to be known) had a virtual monopoly of net-making, with a factory on its own premises and numerous outworkers. Their braiding room was a long gallery at the top of their building in Fish Dock Road, in which the women worked standing either side of the wooden frames. This photograph was taken by Roland Burton in the early 1950s.

Young braiders in party mood at Cosalt's braiding rooms in the late 1930s. The tall dark-haired girl seated in the middle of the front row is Clara Emma Fisher.

George Watson and Joe Chester repairing a damaged trawl net at Beeley and Sleight's net store in the 1930s.

A girl braiding at Cosalt's works in 1953, holding the braiding needle which carried the twine in her right hand, and the spool, the size of which determined the gauge of the net, in her left. The tub on her right is piled with needles filled for her use; one of the more tedious chores for the children of outworkers was filling their mother's needles while she braided.

Waves breaking at high water against the industrial workshops on the Humber Bank, *c*. 1900.

Ice on the quayside waiting to be loaded into a cod-smack. Moored in front of the smack is the *Taurus*, built in 1883, sister-ship of the *Aries* and *Zodiac*, and one of the very first of the steam trawlers.

Ice made commercially in the 1920s by the Grimsby Ice Company being transported along a conveyor above the Pontoon (above) and by chute directly into the fish room of a trawler moored at the quayside (below). The Grimsby Ice Company had one of the largest ice factories in the world; by the 1950s it was capable of producing some 1,250 tons of ice *per day*. A middle water trawler of this period would have taken between 40 and 45 tons of ice to sea with her.

Mr Moyne sewing sacks for ice at the Grimsby Ice Company's factory in Robinson Street East in the mid-1920s.

Grimsby Ice Company worker, 1920s.

Office staff at the Dock Offices on Cleethorpes Road, photographed *c.* 1931–2 by Sid Burton of Grimsby.

The North Eastern Steam Fishing Company's tug-of-war team, winners at both the Friendly and Trade Society's gala, and the Orphan Home gala in 1910.

The Fisherlads' Institute, later known as the Nautical School, in Humber Street, *c.* 1953. As steam took over from sail in the fishing industry, vessels were at sea for longer, penetrating further into higher latitudes, and a more sophisticated knowledge of seamanship and navigational skills was felt to be urgently required. From 1875 the first skippers'

Working on a trawler propeller at Harper Phillips, *c.* 1950.

Casting at Harper Phillips & Co.'s Albion foundry at Eastgate. The company, established in 1870, was making over 20 tons of castings every week even during the Depression, both for the fishing industry and for the Admiralty.

The Dock Estate supported many small engineering workshops and foundries in the early twentieth century. This one, photographed around 1900, is unfortunately unidentified.

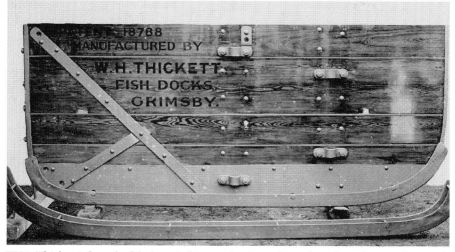

W.H. Thickett's boat-builder's and ship-repairer's yard was based on the Humber Bank at the side of the Fish Docks. This 'trade card', produced probably in the 1920s, shows what appears to be a patented prototype of their 'Fearnaught' reversible otter trawl board. The otter board shown here would be approximately 7 ft 6 in long by 4 ft 6 in wide and immensely heavy, the timbers being separated by iron strips, with an iron 'shoe' to protect the edge of the board as it travelled over the sea-bed.

Construction works on the Dock Estate in the 1950s.

The steam trawler *Leyland* hauled up on the slips of No. 3 Fish Dock, *c.* 1935. The photograph was taken by Stanley Warren.

A Thames barge, the *Leonard Piper* of London, being repaired by shipwrights on Doig's slipway, *c.* 1930. The man on the left is John Bell, the younger man on the steps, Jack Bell.

The aftermath of an expensive mishap . . . *Scarron* hauled up on the slips awaiting the ministrations of E. Bacon's shipwrights.

Inspecting a trawler propeller on the slips at No. 3 Fish Dock, *c.* 1950.

A group of boilermakers on board a trawler moored in the Alexandra Dock for repairs. They are, left to right: Nobby Clarke (from Nottingham), Jimmy Haddock (riveter), Roker Dale (holder-up), Jock Wagstaff (a riveter, who hailed originally from Kilmarnock) and Jack Newman (riveter). The boiler repair shop apparently stood just above Corporation Bridge, which can be seen in the background.

Ship-repairers working for E. Bacon & Co. on board a trawler in the 1930s, relaxing in front of the camera. The young man on the extreme right is Jack Jones.

The 1934 fish dock was built with ten slipways – three hauling and seven dumb – specifically for the new generation of large distant-water trawlers, and were capable of accommodating fishing vessels of up to 1,080 tons displacement. The first steam trawlers of the 1880s were only 90 ft long; by 1934 trawlers of 160 ft in length were being built, and at the outbreak of the Second World War the average length of a new trawler was nearer 180 ft.

The steam trawler *Derby County*, belonging to Consolidated Trawlers, undergoing slipway tests in 1935. She was part of the first batch of 'footballers' ordered by the company, and was built at Smith's Dock in Middlesbrough.

Installing a diesel engine in the *Lucerne*, *c*. 1961–2. The man in the woolly hat at the foot of the ladder is Charlie Hodson, a fitter with Ross Engineers.

Lucerne, a steel-hulled trawler built in Grimsby by J.S. Doig for the Lindsey Steam Fishing Company, flag-bedecked in preparation for her launch in May 1958. After being sold to Kuwait (and then to a scrap merchant), she was rescued from the blowtorch and is still apparently fishing off South Africa.

Jack Evardson, marine fitter and author of *A Fitter's Life*, his very entertaining autobiography, caught in a relaxed moment in a trawler engine room.

Engineers pumping out the *Righto*, one of Sir G.F. Sleight's trawlers, after a mishap in No. 3 Fish Dock.

What became one of the oldest-established shipbuilders and engineers on the docks was founded by John S. Doig, who had works on the Fish Docks (the Strathtay Iron Works) as well as the Royal Dock (the Union Dock Works) where the building and repair of iron ships and boilers was carried out. During the Second World War, as well as patching up casualties and preparing ships used in the D-Day landings, Doig's used vast quantities of oak in the construction of wooden motor minesweepers like this for the Admiralty.

Box girders, 34 ft long, made by Doig's of Grimsby for the Mersey Tunnel, en route through the docks for Liverpool in June 1936.

Doig's work for the Services extended beyond shipbuilding; the curious wooden pyramids being constructed here were used at Donna Nook, further down the coast, for target practice by the RAF.

After the war Doig's continued to build coastal minesweepers for the Admiralty. Both the *Fiskerton* and the *Belton* were built by them in the 1950s; unfortunately, there is not sufficient of its Admiralty number visible to identify which of the duo is being launched here.

James Turner (1847–1931), born and bred in Grimsby, was a tug-boat master on the Humber before the First World War. He was known to many by the honorific title of 'Captain', and by the less respectful as 'Tuggy' Turner. His trademark was the very distinctive overgrown bowler hat that he always wore.

Mr Smedley, Port Missioner for Grimsby until 1899, photographed shortly before the First World War. The Port Missioner had the thankless task of breaking the news to wives and families when fishing vessels were lost.

Riggers at work preparing a trawler for sea in 1959.

The original Tommy Campbell was a smack owner and one of the larger-than-life characters of the late nineteenth-century dock scene. His nephew, another Tommy Campbell, was born in the Campbell villa. On taking control of the business, he recognized that the fishing industry's future lay in steam power and set about selling off his uncle's smack fleet, and re-equipping with steam trawlers. The family name is perpetuated in Campbell's Jetty on the Pontoon; the family home in Abbey Road became the Chest Clinic.

Weelsby Hall, in the early 1900s. This elegant house, which at the time this photograph was taken was outside the Borough of Grimsby and in the separate hamlet of Weelsby, was the home of George Frederick Sleight, fish and ice merchant, auctioneer, fish curer and the largest private steam trawler owner in the world.

SECTION FIVE

Fishermen, on Land and at Sea

Trawlers in the Humber, photographed from the end of Humber Street in New Clee.

The crew of the *Cerealea*, *c.* 1912. The *Cerealea* was built in 1910 and was owned by the Alliance Steam Fishing Company.

The *Woodbury*'s crew and their dog relaxing in port just before the First World War.

Frederick Partis, trawlerman, on board ship at Grimsby in the mid-1930s. When not at sea, he lived in Mangle Street, in the heart of the Grimsby fishing community at New Clee.

Frederick Partis in later life. The 'corn-cob' pipe was said to be a favourite with fishermen.

The *Griffin* steaming off to the North Sea fishing grounds, *c.* 1912. Many of the small smack owners were banding together, as sail gave way to steam at the end of the nineteenth century, and purchasing one or more steam vessels. *Griffin* was an example of this process, being owned by one J. Mackrill 'and others'. Eventually, either one of the partners would become dominant and a limited company created, or the partnership would be subsumed into one or another of the larger groups that had formed.

William Garthwaite took this photograph of the *Camenes* and her ship's boat sailing into the Humber at the end of the nineteenth century.

The crew of the *Grand Fleet*, photographed in the early 1920s.

In 1910 Tom Wing, the newly elected Radical/Labour Member of Parliament for Grimsby, was taken on a fishing trip to the Faeroes in the trawler *Cyrano*, which belonged to Sir Alec Black. The exercise was much derided by his political opponents as a publicity stunt; what his fishermen hosts made of it is not recorded. The voyage was, not surprisingly, extensively photographed; Wing, in the Homburg hat, is pictured above, before sailing, and below, standing knee-deep in fish, tying the cod-end under the critical eye of skipper Sid Cunningham.

Shooting the net over the side on the steam trawler *Loyal* in the 1950s. To 'shoot', or begin fishing, the ship is stopped, the otter boards lifted on the winch and put over the side, and the body of the net and the cod-ends manhandled overboard.

Hauling in the net. The photograph was taken by Jack Jones, a trainee shipwright with Bacon's in the late 1920s. As part of their general training, Bacon's sent their workers to sea on a 'pleasure trip' for the experience.

The Great Grimsby Ice Company's ketch-rigged cod-smack *Hibernia*, racing up the Humber to Grimsby in 1891.

The steam trawler *King Athelstan* heading into port, *c.* 1910. She was built in 1899 at Grimsby for Monarch Steam Fishing. The company was bought out after crashing in 1906 by Consolidated Fisheries, who kept on Monarch's crown emblem seen at the top of her funnel. The photograph was taken by local photographer William Garthwaite.

The ship's cook of the long liner *St Keverne*, photographed in the 1930s. Like many trawlermen, he is wearing 'Fearnought' trousers – loose fitting, button-fronted garments that provided a level of protection from cold and damp.

Verdun Willoughby, mate, and Harry Stratton in the fish room of the trawler *Rose of England*, photographed in 1950. By this time she was a fairly venerable vessel, having been built by Cochrane's at Selby in 1909. She survived until 1961, when, after over fifty years at sea, she was sold for scrap.

Thomas Tompion, one of the new post-war generation of diesel trawlers, undergoing her sea trials on 8 May 1950. Built by Cook, Welton and Gemmel of Beverley, she became one of Grimsby's best-known trawlers (below) but was transferred to Hull owners in 1958, when she was renamed *Stella Procyon* and in 1965, *Ross Procyon*. She was scrapped in 1968.

Releasing the fish from the cod-end. The cod-end on a North Sea trawler such as this would be about 20 ft in length, and secured by a length of manila rope. When the catch has been brought aboard, the line is carefully untied, until only two or three turns remain on the knot, and is then jerked sharply, as shown in the photograph, releasing a cascade of fish into the fish pounds on deck.

Crew members sorting fish in the pounds on the trawler *Buffalo* in 1926.

Percy Burto, the trimmer on the *Natal* in 1934. The trimmer's duties included shovelling coal, trimming the paraffin and navigation lamps, pulling the ashes from the boiler and shooting them over the side, and generally performing the less skilled tasks for the rest of the crew.

A fine ling being held up for Jack Jones to record during his 1920s pleasure trip.

Washing down the decks on the *Buffalo*, 1928.
The fish were gutted on deck and by the time the
men had worked through the catch they would be
ankle-deep in offal, blood and fish scales.

Attending to the nets on the *Orpheus* in the
1930s. Sid Cunningham jun. is on the left.

As part of the intensely resented reparations paid by Germany to the Allies after the First World War, new trawlers were built in German shipyards for British owners. The *Northern Sun*, seen here sailing out of Grimsby, was one such vessel, built by Rickmers Werft at Bremerhaven in 1936, and owned by Northern Trawlers Ltd. She was scrapped in 1966.

Aston Villa, one of the third generation of coal-burning 'footballers' purchased by Consolidated Trawlers from Smith's Dock Company at Middlesbrough. She is seen here in No. 3 Fish Dock, shortly after sailing down to the port from Middlesbrough in 1937. Like many trawlers, she was requisitioned by the Admiralty after the outbreak of the Second World War, and on 3 May 1940, with seven other Grimsby trawlers, was sunk by German aircraft during the battle for Norway.

Sharks are relatively common in northern waters. This creature was landed by the Grimsby trawler *Emperor* in the late 1890s. The two apprentice-boys look slightly overawed by their catch.

A crew member of the steam trawler *Premier* preparing to gut a small shark, c. 1898.

When it became obvious that war with Germany was imminent, the Admiralty either bought up or requisitioned some 250 Grimsby trawlers, converting the Arctic vessels for anti-submarine work, and the smaller vessels for minesweeping and other duties. The *Lacennia*, seen here en route from Loch Ewe to Iceland, was requisitioned in October 1939. Her bridge was raised, and she was equipped with minesweeping gear and the single 12-pounder gun seen on her bows. She worked the area from Iceland to the east coast of England from the beginning of the war until February 1946, when she was returned to her owners.

Below decks on the minesweeper *Ben Meidie*, March 1943. The trawler had first been requisitioned by the Admiralty in 1917, and was required for service once again in January 1940. She survived that conflict also, and was finally returned to her owners in March 1946.

The crew of the *St Keverne* line-fishing in the 1930s. The traditional method of catching fish in the North Sea was the use of long lines. A cod-smack would carry some 16 dozen lines, each 39 fathoms long, with short, interconnected lines (the 'snoods') which carried the baited hooks. The steam liners like *St Keverne* being built at the end of the century carried considerably more.

A Grimsby steam liner, *c.* 1912. The young man on the left, in the white 'Fearnought' trousers, was Richard Newland, who was apprenticed to Crampin's at the time.

Mr A. Finch 'tricking up' in preparation for shooting the lines. Shooting started at midnight, and had generally ended by 4 a.m., and at daybreak the liner would turn back on its course, hooking the fish – usually cod or ling – as it went. The great enemies of the line-fishermen were dogfish, a generic name for a variety of small sharks. These ferocious creatures have a keen sense of smell, and fish caught on the baited hooks of a long line were easy prey. Often the fishermen found only the cleaned skeletons or heads attached to the hooks when the lines were hauled in.

The coal-burner *Hawkins* setting off for the North Sea and beyond.

Cleaning gutted fish in the washing pounds of the *Premier* in the late 1890s.

One of the greatest hazards to trawlers in Arctic waters was icing. It could be expected when the air temperature – and hence the ship's surface – was below the freezing point of the sea, and the wind was of sufficient strength to blow spray from the wave crests which would adhere to the ship. In a Force 10 gale, this would happen extremely quickly. The added weight caused ships to lose stability as they became top heavy, and steering could become impossible. Any build-up of ice would also affect the efficiency of radar, aerials and compass, exacerbating the danger. The only remedies were de-icing with steam or manually chopping with an ice-axe, an extremely hazardous and often futile endeavour in a full gale on a pitching deck. The photograph to the left shows the *Grand Fleet*, that to the right an unnamed trawler in the Barents Sea in 1949. They survived – many did not.

Skipper Peter Woldemar relaxing with pipe and feathered friends on his ship in the 1890s.

Acknowledgements

I am grateful to the Director of Leisure and Economic Development, Great Grimsby Borough Council, for permission to use photographs from the collections of the Great Grimsby Museum and Heritage Service. Many of the photographs are from the W.E.R. Hallgarth Collection, given to the Borough in 1979. I should also like to thank the following people who have so generously made available to the museum service over the past decade photographs included in this book:

Mr D. Armstrong ARPS • Mrs Baker • Mr J. Bell • Mrs J. Bond • Mrs Borrill
Mr Brough • Mrs R. Burton • Mr D. Campbell • Mr E. Coles • Mrs Collinson
Mr A. Credland • Mr Dawson • Mr J. Evardson • Mr A. Finch
Mr Fountain • Mrs P. Francis • Mr Gaiger • Mr A. Hodson • Mrs V. Howdle
Humberside Police • Mr Ingrams • Mr J. Jones • Mr Lister
Mrs H. Loaring • Mrs Mamafesk • Mr McKie • Mr C. Mercer
Mr G. Mosley • Mr Niles • Mrs Read • Mrs Smith • Mr Sullivan
Mr E. Sveinsson • Mrs Swift • Mrs Swinburn • Mr Tuck
Viking TV, Denmark • Mr J. Wakelin • Mrs Watkinson • Mr E. Watson
Mr A. Whittleton • Mr V. Willoughby • Mr Willows • Miss Wilson.

I thank also my friends and colleagues at Grimsby for all their help and advice, particularly Ray Spink and Cyril Springhall, who fielded my endless questions about fishing, and Chris Volley, who suffered my depredations to the photograph library with great patience.